Focus ENGLISH

Anthology 6
Text extracts

Written and compiled by
Chris Buckton and **Pie Corbett**
with contributions from **Gill Matthews**

Series Editor: **Leonie Bennett**

Heinemann

Heinemann Educational Publishers
Halley Court, Jordan Hill, Oxford OX2 8EJ
a division of Reed Educational & Professional Publishing Limited

Heinemann is a registered trademark of Reed Educational & Professional Publishing Limited

OXFORD MELBOURNE AUCKLAND IBADAN JOHANNESBURG
GABORONE BLANTYRE PORTSMOUTH NH (USA) CHICAGO

© Reed Educational and Professional Publishing 1998

The moral right of the proprietor has been asserted.

First published 1998

02 01 00 99 98
10 9 8 7 6 5 4 3 2

All rights reserved. No part of this publication may be reproduced or transmitted in any form, or by any means, electronic or mechanical, including photocopy, recording or any information storage and retrieval system without permission in writing from the publishers.

British Library Cataloguing in Publication Data
A catalogue record for this book is available from the British Library.

ISBN 0 435 107577   single copy
ISBN 0 435 106457   6 copy pack

Designed by Celia Floyd
Colour repro by Ambassador
Printed in Spain

Contents

Unit	Focus/range	Page
1 Macbeth 1	modern retelling	4
2 Macbeth 2	Shakespeare play	7
3 Capturing Animals	writer's journal	10
4 The Warm and the Cold	work of an established poet	12
5 James and the Giant Peach	novel and film script	14
6 Two Orphan Flower Girls	Victorian report	18
7 Bleak House	classic novel	20
8 Judgement Day	newspaper article	24
9 The Rabbit's Advice	work of an established poet	26
10 Shall we go to Africa?	author's point of view	28
11 Antarctica	fact/opinion	32
12 The Balaclava Story 1	comic effect/plot structure	34
13 The Balaclava Story 2	comic effect/plot structure	37
14 Jabberwocky	nonsense poetry	38
15 The Stove Haunting	ghost story/flashback	40
16 Kennings Cat	poetic forms	44
17 Waterways Museum	information leaflet	46
18 The Present Takers	genre comparison I	48
19 Struggling to be Real	genre comparison II	52
20 Cover blurbs	story summary	56
21 Anne Fine	author study	58
22 The Write Stuff	autobiography	61
23 From 'rash' to 'sprain'	medical encyclopaedia	64
24 Small Dawn Song	comparison of significant poets	66
25 Evacuation	explanation of process	68
26 Wartime	stories with similar theme	70
27 Haiku Bestiary	sequence of poems	74
28 The Bogeyman	picture stories	76
29 This is Just to Say	poetry	80

UNIT 1 Macbeth 1

Meeting the witches

1 Right at the beginning, Shakespeare sets the mood of the story. There is thunder and lightning and three witches appear. They announce that they will meet again on a heath to greet Macbeth. Then they disappear into the 'filthy air' as mysteriously as they arrived. What terrible things, the audience wonders, will they say to Macbeth?

Macbeth and Banquo, co-leaders of the Scottish army, are returning from battle when they meet the three witches on a
10 heath. The witches prophesy that Macbeth will become Thane of Cawdor and, later, king. Soon afterwards, messengers arrive with the news that Macbeth has been made Thane of Cawdor. Macbeth begins to consider the possibility of becoming king! There is a chance that King Duncan might choose Macbeth, a cousin, to be king after him. But Macbeth's hopes are dashed when Duncan names his son, Malcolm, as his successor.

For a moment, Macbeth imagines killing Duncan. Then he dismisses the horrid thought. We know though that he is now becoming ambitious.

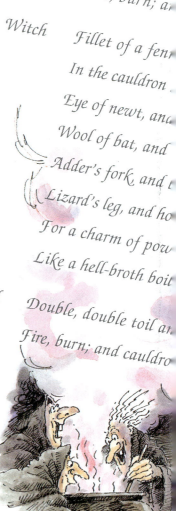

All Double, doub
Fire, burn; a
Witch Fillet of a fen
In the cauldron
Eye of newt, and
Wool of bat, and
Adder's fork, and
Lizard's leg, and ho
For a charm of pow
Like a hell-broth boil
All Double, double toil a
Fire, burn; and cauldro

4

Lady Macbeth plans a murder

Meanwhile, at home in their castle, Lady Macbeth has received a letter from her husband. In it he tells her about the witches' prophesies.

At that moment, a messenger arrives telling her the King is about to visit. She realises that this is the perfect opportunity to kill him. She makes up her mind that the murder must be committed that night. When Macbeth arrives at the castle ahead of the King, she tells him she has arranged everything and persuades him to kill the King.

Macbeth has fears and doubts

Duncan, the King, arrives with his two sons, Malcolm and Donalbain. Lady Macbeth welcomes him in a most friendly way. Macbeth, however, has doubts about the murder and he tells Lady Macbeth that he has changed his mind.

Lady Macbeth's anger

Lady Macbeth is furious. She accuses him of being a coward for not having the courage to do what he wants. She angrily says that she would kill her own child if that was what she had promised to do. Her feelings are so strong that Macbeth gives in completely. And he agrees to go ahead as she has planned.

Macbeth sees a bloodstained dagger

Alone in his room, Macbeth has a terrible vision of a dagger which he tries to grasp but cannot get hold of. He tells himself that he is imagining things because he is afraid. But he keeps seeing the dagger – the second time it has blood on it. Then he hears a bell ring. This is Lady Macbeth's signal. He now has to kill Duncan.

How Macbeth murders Duncan

Lady Macbeth has made sure that Duncan's guards are asleep by putting drugs in their drink. She has also put out two daggers for Macbeth to use. She keeps watch outside while Macbeth enters the King's chambers. When he comes out he is staggering. His arms are covered with blood and he is still holding the blood-stained daggers. It is obvious that Macbeth has gone to pieces. He is overcome by guilt and horror at what he has done. She tells him to pull himself together – to take the daggers back and smear the guards with blood. But Macbeth is in such a state of shock that he cannot. Lady Macbeth quickly replaces the daggers near the guards herself and sends Macbeth to change into his nightgown, so that he can pretend he has been asleep.

Questions

1. Who are the main characters in the story?
2. Who do you think is most to blame for Duncan's murder – Macbeth, Lady Macbeth or the witches?
3. How do Macbeth's feelings change during the story?

You might like to find out what happens to Macbeth in the end. If so, you could look in the library for the story or watch a video of the play.

UNIT 2 — Macbeth 2

From: MACBETH ACT 2, SCENE 2

[Enter Macbeth, carrying two bloodstained daggers]

LADY MACBETH

My husband!

MACBETH

I have done the deed. Didst thou not hear a noise?

LADY MACBETH

I heard the owl scream and the cricket's cry.
Did not you speak?

MACBETH   When?

LADY MACBETH   Now.

MACBETH   As I descended?

LADY MACBETH

Ay.

MACBETH

Hark!
Who lies i' the second chamber?

LADY MACBETH   Donalbain.

MACBETH [*Looks at his hands.*]

This is a sorry sight.

LADY MACBETH

A foolish thought, to say a sorry sight.

MACBETH

There's one did laugh in's sleep, and one cried 'Murder!'
That they did wake each other. I stood and heard them.
But they did say their prayers and addressed them
Again to sleep.

LADY MACBETH   There are two lodged together.

MACBETH
> One cried 'God bless us' and 'Amen' the other,
> As they had seen me with these hangman's hands.
> Listening their fear I could not say 'Amen'
> When they did say 'God bless us.'

LADY MACBETH
> Consider it not so deeply.

MACBETH
> But wherefore could not I pronounce 'Amen'?
> I had most need of blessing, and 'Amen'
> Stuck in my throat.

LADY MACBETH   These deeds must not be thought
> After these ways; so, it will make us mad.

MACBETH
> Methought I heard a voice cry, 'Sleep no more!
> Macbeth does murder sleep' – the innocent sleep,
> Sleep that knits up the ravelled sleave of care,
> The death of each day's life, sore labour's bath,
> Balm of hurt minds, great nature's second course,
> Chief nourisher in life's feast.

LADY MACBETH   What do you mean?

MACBETH
> Still it cried 'Sleep no more' to all the house.
> 'Glamis hath murdered sleep, and therefore Cawdor
> Shall sleep no more, Macbeth shall sleep no more.'

LADY MACBETH
> Who was it that thus cried? Why, worthy thane,
> You do unbend your noble strength, to think
> So brain-sickly of things. Go, get some water,
> And wash this filthy witness from your hand.
> Why did you bring these daggers from the place?
> They must lie there. Go, carry them and smear
> The sleepy grooms with blood.

MACBETH   I'll go no more.
   I am afraid to think what I have done;
   Look on't again I dare not.
   LADY MACBETH   Infirm of purpose!
50   Give me the daggers. The sleeping and the dead
   Are but as pictures. 'Tis the eye of childhood
   That fears a painted devil. If he do bleed,
   I'll gild the faces of the grooms withal,
   For it must seem their guilt.   *Exit*
         Knock within
   MACBETH   Whence is that knocking?
   How is't with me when every noise appals me?
   What hands are here! Ha - they pluck out mine eyes!
   Will all great Neptune's ocean wash this blood
   Clean from my hand? No, this my hand will rather
60   The multitudinous seas incarnadine,
   Making the green one red.
         Enter Lady Macbeth
   LADY MACBETH
   My hands are of your colour; but I shame
   To wear a heart so white.
         Knock within
                        I hear a knocking
   At the south entry. Retire we to our chamber.
   A little water clears us of this deed;
   How easy is it then!
                        William Shakespeare

Questions

1   a) Duncan's two sons woke up and said their prayers (line 16). What had woken them?
    b) Why did '*Amen*' stick in Macbeth's throat? (line 25)
2   How does Shakespeare show us what Macbeth and his wife are feeling at this moment in the play?
3   a) Why does Lady Macbeth tell Macbeth to put the daggers next to the grooms and smear them with blood? (line 44)
    b) Why can't Macbeth do it?

UNIT 3 Capturing Animals

1   . . .the rules, to begin with, are very simple. Words that live are those which we hear, like *click* or *chuckle* or which we see, like *freckled* or *veined*, or which we taste, like *vinegar* or *sugar*, or touch like *prickle* or *oily*, or smell, like *tar* or *onion*. Words which belong directly to one of the five senses. Or words which act and seem to use their muscles like *flick* or *balance*.

But immediately things become more difficult. *Click* not only gives you a sound, it gives you the notion of a sharp movement . . . such as your tongue makes in saying 'click'. It also gives you the feel
10 of something light and brittle, like a snapping twig. Heavy things do not click, nor do soft bendable ones.

In the same way, *tar* not only smells strongly. It is sticky to touch, with a particular thick and choking stickiness. Also it moves, when it is soft, like a black snake, and has a beautiful black gloss.

So it is with most words. They belong to several of the senses at once, as if each one had eyes, ears and tongue, or ears and fingers and a body to move with. It is this little goblin in a word which is its life and its poetry and it is this goblin which the poet has to have under control.

Well, you will say, this is hopeless. How do you control all that? When the words are pouring out, how can you be sure that you do not have one of these side meanings of the word *feathers* getting all stuck up with one of the side meanings of the word treacle a few words later. . .

Luckily, you do not have to bother about it as long as you do one thing. . . That one thing is, imagine what you are writing about. See it and live it. Do not think it up laboriously, as if you were working out mental arithmetic. Just look at it, touch it, smell it, listen to it, turn yourself into it. When you do this, the words look after themselves, like magic. If you do this you do not have to bother about commas or full-stops or that sort of thing. . .

So you keep going as long as you can, then look back and see what you have written. After a bit of practice . . . and after telling yourself you are going to use any old word that comes into your head so long as it seems right at the moment of writing it down, you will surprise yourself. You will read back through what you have written and you will get a shock. You will have captured a spirit, a creature.

Ted Hughes

Questions

1. a) Find three examples of words which 'live' according to Ted Hughes. (first paragraph)
   b) Why do these words live?
2. *most words . . . belong to several of the senses at once* (lines 15-16).
   In what ways does the word *tar* belong to several senses? (third paragraph)
3. What advice does Ted Hughes give about punctuation?
4. Do you think he is suggesting that you should write slowly or quickly?
5. *imagine what you are writing about. . . Just look at it, touch it, smell it, listen to it, turn yourself into it* (lines 26-9).
   What do you think Ted Hughes means by this?

UNIT 4 The Warm and the Cold

Freezing dusk is closing
Like a slow trap of steel
On trees and roads and hills and all
That can no longer feel.
But the carp is in its depth
Like a planet in its heaven.
And the badger in its bedding
Like a loaf in the oven.
And the butterfly in its mummy
Like a viol in its case.
And the owl in its feathers
Like a doll in its lace.

Freezing dusk has tightened
Like a nut screwed tight
On the starry aeroplane
Of the soaring night.
But the trout is in its hole
Like a chuckle in a sleeper.
The hare strays down the highway
Like a root going deeper.
The snail is dry in the outhouse
Like a seed in a sunflower.
The owl is pale on the gatepost
Like a clock on its tower.

Moonlight freezes the shaggy world
   Like a mammoth of ice –
The past and the future
   Are the jaws of a steel vice.
     But the cod is in the tide-rip
        Like a key in a purse.
   The deer are on the bare-blown hill
     Like smiles on a nurse.
   The flies are behind the plaster
     Like the lost score of a jig.
Sparrows are in the ivy-clump
   Like money in a pig.

        Such a frost
          The flimsy moon
            Hast lost her wits.

        A star falls.

       The sweating farmers
       Turn in their sleep
         Like oxen on spits.

Ted Hughes

Questions

1. What time of day is suggested by the first line in each of the first three verses?
2. What time of year is it? Which words and phrases tell us?
3. How are the animals, in spite of the weather?
4. Why is the poem called *The Warm and the Cold*?

UNIT 5 James and the Giant Peach

From the book

1   Until he was four years old, James Henry Trotter had a happy life. He lived peacefully with his mother and father in a beautiful house beside the sea. There were always plenty of other children for him to play with, and there was the sandy beach for him to run about on, and the ocean to paddle in. It was the perfect life for a small boy.

Then, one day, James's mother and father went to London
10 to do some shopping, and there a terrible thing happened. Both of them suddenly got eaten up (in full daylight, mind you, and on a crowded street) by an enormous angry rhinoceros which had escaped from the London Zoo.

Now this, as you can well imagine, was a rather nasty experience for two such gentle parents. But in the long run it was far nastier for James than it was for them. *Their* troubles were all over in a jiffy. They were dead and gone in thirty-five seconds flat. Poor James, on the other hand, was still very much alive, and all at once he found himself alone and frightened in a
20 vast unfriendly world. The lovely house by the seaside had to be sold immediately, and the little boy, carrying nothing but a small suitcase containing a pair of pyjamas and a toothbrush, was sent away to live with his two aunts.

Their names were Aunt Sponge and Aunt Spiker, and I am sorry to say that they were both really horrible people. They were selfish and lazy and cruel, and right from the beginning they started beating poor James for almost no reason at all. They never called him by his real name, but always referred to him as 'you disgusting little beast' or 'you filthy nuisance' or 'you
30 miserable creature', and they certainly never gave him any toys to play with or any picture books to look at. His room was as bare as a prison cell.

They lived – Aunt Sponge and Aunt Spiker, and now James as well – in a queer ramshackle house on the top of a high hill in the south of England. The hill was so high that from almost anywhere in the garden James could look down and see for miles and miles across a marvellous landscape of woods and fields; and on a very clear day, if he looked in the right direction, he could see a tiny grey dot far away on the horizon, which was the house that he used to live in with his beloved mother and father. And just beyond that, he could see the ocean itself – a long thin streak of blackish-blue, like a line of ink, beneath the rim of the sky.

But James was never allowed to go down off the top of that hill. Neither Aunt Sponge nor Aunt Spiker could ever be bothered to take him out herself, not even for a small walk or a picnic, and he certainly wasn't permitted to go alone...

Aunt Sponge was enormously fat and very short. She had small piggy eyes, a sunken mouth, and one of those white flabby faces that looked exactly as though it had been boiled. She was like a great white soggy overboiled cabbage. Aunt Spiker, on the other hand, was lean and tall and bony, and she wore steel-rimmed spectacles that fixed on to the end of her nose with a clip. She had a screeching voice and long wet narrow lips, and whenever she got angry or excited, little flecks of spit would come shooting out of her mouth as she talked.

Roald Dahl

From the screenplay of the film

[TITLE SEQUENCE]

5   CLOSE ON THE FRONT DOOR OF THE AUNTS' RAMSHACKLE HOUSE. The door flies open and A WOODEN CHEST ON WHEELS rolls out, the word 'TOYS' emblazoned across its front. TILT UP to find James pushing the toy chest which is filled with rakes, hoes, shovels, etc. He pushes it down the barren rocky hill to...

6   A SCRAGGLY PEACH TREE WITH NO FRUIT AND NO LEAVES.

    James swings a pick axe at the dirt beneath the tree. The film's title appears beside this tableau:

JAMES AND THE GIANT PEACH

7   OMIT

8   OMIT

9   James polishes the grille of a 1936 Jaguar until it is shining like new! PULL BACK to reveal the rest of the car is all rust.

10 OMIT

11 James pulls laundry from a basket and hangs it on a clothes line to dry. First he pulls up Sponge's extra large girdle, then, like scarves out of a magician's hat, he pulls out Spiker's long skinny gown — which keeps coming, and coming, and coming ...

12 James dusts a photo of Spiker and Sponge. PULL BACK to find that the whole wall is covered with various photos of them.

13 EXT. AUNT'S HOUSE/BENEATH THE PEACH TREE - MORNING

16

A LARGE BUTTERFLY lands on a table beside a
pitcher of lemonade. SPLAT! – a hand-carved
flyswatter squashes it into oblivion. (O.S. –
we hear the SOUND of an axe CHOPPING WOOD).

     SPIKER
  Ew. Wouldn't want one of those
  nesting in your knickers.

With a grimace, SPIKER flicks the flyswatter and
the bug flies off. It soars past Sponge who's so
absorbed with her reflection in her long-handled
mirror, she doesn't notice.

     SPONGE
 I LOOK AND SMELL, I DO DECLARE,
  AS LOVELY AS A ROSE
 JUST FEAST YOUR EYES UPON MY FACE,
  OBSERVE MY SHAPELY NOSE!
 BEHOLD MY HEAVENLY SILKY LOCKS!
  AND IF I TAKE OFF BOTH MY SOCKS
YOU'LL SEE MY DAINTY TOES!

Questions

1. a) What sort of life does James have with his aunts?
   b) How does the screenplay give us this information?
2. a) What do the aunts look like? Find words and phrases in the novel extract which describe them.
   b) How does the screenplay give us this information?
3. Why do you think the screenplay doesn't include James' parents being eaten by a rhinoceros?

UNIT 6 Two Orphan Flower Girls

1   Of these girls the elder was fifteen and the younger eleven. Both were clad in old, but not torn, dark print frocks, hanging so closely, and yet so loosely, about them as to show the deficiency of under-clothing; they wore old broken black chip bonnets. The older sister (or rather half-sister) had a pair of old worn-out shoes on her feet, the younger was barefoot, but trotted along, in a gait at once quick and feeble as if the soles of her little feet were impervious, like horn, to the roughness of the road.

   The elder girl has no pretensions to prettiness except in
10 having tolerably good eyes. Her complexion was somewhat pinched. The younger child had a round, chubby, and even rosy face, and quite a healthful look.

   They lived in one of the streets near Drury-lane. They were inmates of a house inhabited by street-sellers and street-labourers. The room they occupied was large, and one dim candle lighted it so insufficiently that it seemed to exaggerate the dimensions. The walls were bare and discoloured with damp. The furniture consisted of a crazy table and a few chairs, and in the centre of the room was an old four-post bedstead of the
20 larger size. This bed was occupied nightly by the two sisters and their brother, a lad just turned thirteen. In a sort of recess in a corner of the room was the decency of an old curtain – or something equivalent, for I could hardly see in the dimness – and behind this was, I presume, the bed of the married couple.

The younger of the two girls, sketched at the time the report was written (1851).

The three children paid 2s. a week for the room, the tenant, an Irishman out of work, paying 2s. 9d., but the furniture was his, and his wife aided the children in their trifle of washing, mended their clothes, where such a thing was possible, and such like. The husband was absent at the time of my visit,
30 but the wife seemed of a better stamp, judging by her appearance, and by her refraining from any direct, or even indirect, way of begging.

Henry Mayhew

Questions

1. Do you think the author's style in this extract is formal or informal? Why do you think that?
2. Do you think we are given facts about the girls or are they the author's opinions? Why do you think that?
3. What impression do you get of the girls' lives?
4. Find three phrases that make you think that this piece was written a long time ago.

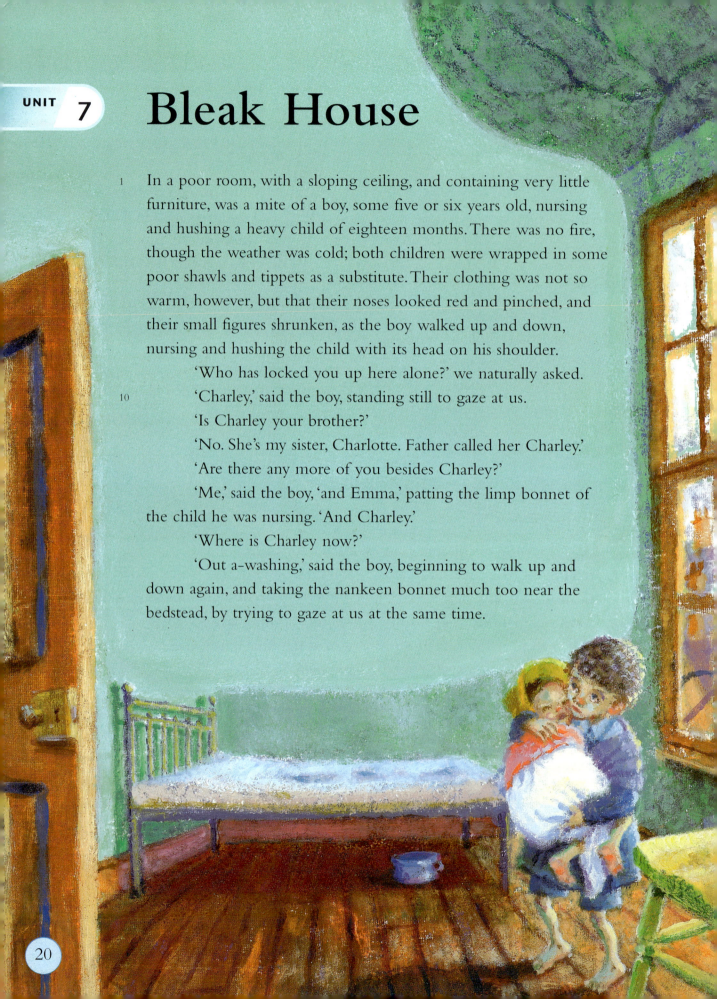

UNIT 7 Bleak House

1   In a poor room, with a sloping ceiling, and containing very little furniture, was a mite of a boy, some five or six years old, nursing and hushing a heavy child of eighteen months. There was no fire, though the weather was cold; both children were wrapped in some poor shawls and tippets as a substitute. Their clothing was not so warm, however, but that their noses looked red and pinched, and their small figures shrunken, as the boy walked up and down, nursing and hushing the child with its head on his shoulder.

'Who has locked you up here alone?' we naturally asked.

10   'Charley,' said the boy, standing still to gaze at us.

'Is Charley your brother?'

'No. She's my sister, Charlotte. Father called her Charley.'

'Are there any more of you besides Charley?'

'Me,' said the boy, 'and Emma,' patting the limp bonnet of the child he was nursing. 'And Charley.'

'Where is Charley now?'

'Out a-washing,' said the boy, beginning to walk up and down again, and taking the nankeen bonnet much too near the bedstead, by trying to gaze at us at the same time.

We were looking at one another, and at these two children, when there came into the room a very little girl, childish in figure but shrewd and older-looking in the face – pretty-faced too – wearing a womanly sort of bonnet much too large for her, and drying her bare arms on a womanly sort of apron. Her fingers were white and wrinkled with washing, and the soap-suds were yet smoking which she wiped off her arms. But for this, she might have been a child, playing at washing, and imitating a poor working-woman with a quick observation of the truth.

She had come running from some place in the neighbourhood, and had made all the haste she could. Consequently, though she was very light, she was out of breath, and could not speak at first, as she stood panting, and wiping her arms, and looking quietly at us.

'O, here's Charley!' said the boy.

The child he was nursing, stretched forth its arms, and cried out to be taken by Charley. The little girl took it, in a womanly sort of manner belonging to the apron and the bonnet, and stood looking at us over the burden that clung to her most affectionately.

'Is it possible,' whispered my guardian, as we put a chair for the little creature, and got her to sit down with her load: the boy keeping close to her, holding to her apron, 'that this child works for the rest? Look at this! For God's sake look at this!'

It was a thing to look at. The three children close together, and two of them relying solely on the third, and the third so young and yet with an air of age and steadiness that sat so strangely on the childish figure.

'Charley, Charley!' said my guardian. 'How old are you?'

'Over thirteen, sir,' replied the child.

'O! What a great age,' said my guardian. 'What a great age, Charley!'

I cannot describe the tenderness with which he spoke to her; half playfully, yet all the more compassionately and mournfully.

'And do you live alone here with these babies, Charley?' said my guardian.

'Yes, sir,' returned the child, looking up into his face with perfect confidence, 'since my father died.'

'And how do you live, Charley? O! Charley,' said my guardian, turning his face away for a moment, 'how do you live?'

'Since father died, sir, I've gone out to work. I'm out washing today.'

'God help you, Charley!' said my guardian. 'You're not tall enough to reach the tub!'

'In pattens I am, sir,' she said quickly. 'I've got a high pair as belonged to mother.'

'And when did mother die? Poor mother!'

'Mother died just after Emma was born,' said the child, glancing at the face upon her bosom. 'Then father said I was to be as good a mother to her as I could. And so I tried. And so I worked at home, and did cleaning and nursing and washing, for a long time before I began to go out. And that's how I know how; don't you see, sir?'

'And do you often go out?'

'As often as I can,' said Charley, opening her eyes, and smiling, 'because of earning sixpences and shillings!'

'And do you always lock the babies up when you go out?'

'To keep em safe, sir, don't you see?' said Charley. 'Mrs Blinder comes up now and then, and Mr Gridley comes up sometimes, and perhaps I can run in sometimes, and they can play you know, and Tom an't afraid of being locked up, are you, Tom?'

'No-o!' said Tom, stoutly.

'When it comes on dark, the lamps are lighted down in the court, and they show up here quite bright – almost quite bright. Don't they Tom?'

'Yes, Charley,' said Tom, 'almost quite bright.'

'Then he's as good as gold,' said the little creature – O! in such a motherly, womanly way! 'And when Emma's tired, he puts her to bed. And when he's tired he goes to bed himself. And when I come home and light the candle, and has a bit of supper, he sits up again and has it with me. Don't you Tom?'

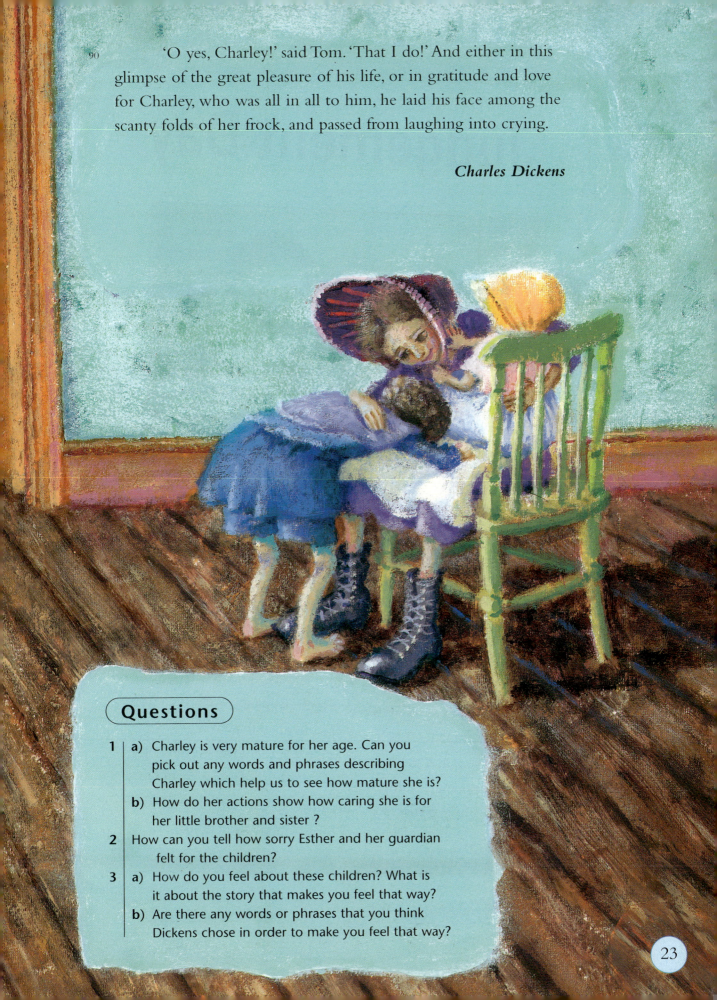

'O yes, Charley!' said Tom. 'That I do!' And either in this glimpse of the great pleasure of his life, or in gratitude and love for Charley, who was all in all to him, he laid his face among the scanty folds of her frock, and passed from laughing into crying.

Charles Dickens

Questions

1. a) Charley is very mature for her age. Can you pick out any words and phrases describing Charley which help us to see how mature she is?
   b) How do her actions show how caring she is for her little brother and sister?
2. How can you tell how sorry Esther and her guardian felt for the children?
3. a) How do you feel about these children? What is it about the story that makes you feel that way?
   b) Are there any words or phrases that you think Dickens chose in order to make you feel that way?

Judgement Day

1   **Last summer, *10.15* launched the hunt for two book-loving teenagers to help judge the 1997 Whitbread Children's Book of the Year. Guy Walters got wordy with the winners.**
Are we a nation of story-guzzling bookworms? You may remember that a while back, we asked readers to send in reviews of their favourite books, and the writers of the two best reviews would join the Whitbread panel. Well, the office was swamped – it took ages just to open the envelopes. However, after many hours of sifting, the novelist Anne Fine
10 and I came up with two winners: Maria Adey, 12, from Great Bardfield in Essex, and Sally Inwood, 14, from Buckover in Gloucestershire. They were sent 15 books which they had to read within three weeks.

Last week, Maria (pictured top left) and Sally (top right) joined their fellow judges in London to work out which were their favourite four. Maria confessed that she hadn't had time to read all the books. 'Because I'm at boarding school I even had to read with a torch in bed at night,' she laughed. However Sally had managed to finish them, 'Although I'm not too sure how,' she admitted. Luckily both are keen readers, and, unsurprisingly, neither watch much TV.

20 The girls were to have a long day ahead. The discussions were held in secret, but I managed to drag them out of the meeting after three hours. 'So far, it's been really fun,' said Maria, 'We've been completely included in all of it.' So what qualities were the girls looking for? 'I want to read a book I can identify with,' said Sally. 'And that makes me think. Of course, it has to be enjoyable too.'

Maria said she looks for a plot, 'but I like to have an extra twist that makes it more exciting as well as it being a book I can read again and again.' Sally and Maria both said they'd had their minds changed by the judges, but they denied that they had been walked over. 'It was good for us,' said Sally. 'It made me
30 start to think of the books in a way I might not have done.' 'Most of us had the same feelings about the books,' said Maria. 'And it was not as if anybody was on their own in liking a book.'

The meeting looked as if it was going to last all day. At that stage they still seemed perky, but I expect after a few hours more of debate they may have wilted.

The four books they selected will be judged by another panel, but come January, when the award is announced, Sally and Maria will be up there on stage to receive a well-earned round of applause.

The Times 25.10.97

Questions

1. What book award is this article about?
2. Who is the novelist mentioned in the article?
3. What qualities are the girls looking for in a book?
4. Why do you think the opening paragraph is in bold print?
5. Where does it tell us who wrote this article?

The Rabbit's Advice

The Rabbit's Advice

1   I have been away too long.
    Some of you think I am only a nursery tale,
    One which you've grown out of.
    Or perhaps you saw a movie and laughed at my ears
    But rather envied my carrot.
    I must tell you that I exist.

    I'm a puff of wool leaping across a field,
    Quick to all noises,
    Smelling my burrow of safety.
10 I am easily frightened. A bird
    Is tame compared to me.
    Perhaps you have seen my fat white cousin who sits,
    Constantly twitching his nose,
    Behind bars in a hutch at the end of a garden.
    If not, imagine those nights when you lie awake
    Afraid to turn over, afraid
    Of night and dawn and sleep.
    Terror is what I am made
    Of partly, partly of speed.

20 But I am a figure of fun.
    I have no dignity
    Which means I am never free.
    So, when you are frightened or being teased, think of
    My twitching whiskers, my absurd white puff of a tail,
    Of all that I mean by 'me'
    And my ludicrous craving for love.

The Hedgehog's Explanation

I move very slowly,
I would like to be friendly,
Yet my prickly back has a look of danger. You might
Suppose I were ready for war or at least a fight
With a cat on the wall, a gather of birds, but no,
My prickles damage nobody, so you

Must be gentle with me, you with your huge shadow,
Your footsteps like claps of thunder.
The terrible touch of your hands.
10 Listen to me: I am a ball of fear,
Terror is what I know best,
What I live with and dream about.
Put out a saucer of milk for me,
Keep me from roads and cars.
If you want to look after someone,
Take care of me
And give me at least the pretence I am safe and free.

Both these poems are by Elizabeth Jennings.

Questions

1. According to the rabbit, how do most people think of it?
2. What two things does the rabbit say it is made of?
3. Explain, in your own words, the advice given by the rabbit in the last four lines.
4. What two things is the hedgehog explaining?
5. How does the poem make you feel about the hedgehog?

Shall we go to Africa?

From NYAR-UPOKO

1   Shall we go to Africa. . ?
Shall we. . ?

Well then, imagine night. You can shut your eyes if you like. A warm night. Don't be afraid, it isn't dark. Imagine a moon, a full round silver-yellow moon up there shining down on us.

It's not so dark now. Sort of greyish; silver greys, light greys and dark greys. You can make out grey shapes, the shapes of bushes and trees – tall dark feathery eucalyptus trees, rustling in the light breeze. The breeze is warm and brings the sweet scent of night flowers – frangipani.

10 A small shadow moves – a dog, two dogs. No, one dog and its shadow upside-down. Wherever the shadow goes, the dog goes too. The dog sniffs its shadow and the shadow sniffs its dog. Their noses touch for a moment. Pfff! The dog and its shadow move on.

Keep going. We're not quite there yet. This is night in Africa – a full moon night, the time in Africa for telling stories outside.

Now imagine noise – the night in Africa is never silent – lots of noise, noise all around. Millions and millions of insects: busy *dudus*, chizzing and deedling all night long. Some little and others not so little, all night long they never stop telling stories, the noisy *dudus*. And frogs too, always warking. Sometimes a *dudu* chizzes so loud and near, your eardrums humzzz.

We're almost there now. Do you still want to go there. . ?

Well, now imagine two children, a girl and a boy, and their grandma, coming out of the house. 'Here children, come and sit by me,' says Grandma. 'I'll tell you about Nyar-upoko, the love child. Sit here my children, and listen.'

Here we are at last, sitting under the silver-yellow moon, and all round us the everlasting *dudus*.

Grandma sits down slowly on the story stool on the sunset side of the house. 'Ooof! That's good,' she says. 'How this warm wall oils my old bones.'

Her grandchildren, Awiti and Kech, sit cross-legged on the ground next to her. Awiti is two years older than her brother Kech. She is eleven and is in Standard Four at Kamuga Primary School. Kech is in Standard Two and is nine years old.

The silver-grey dog ambles round the compound in the moonshine. It stops to scratch under its armpit and starts hunting a flea.

'Yes, my children,' continues Grandma. 'Nyar-upoko, the girl who lived by tender loving care. But when people hated her, she grew cold and lifeless and floppy like a dead bird. . . Now my child, run off and bring me a stick from the fire to light my pipe with. We old women like our pipes in the evening.'

So Kech runs off into the darkness and comes back with a glowing stick. Grandma lights her long pipe and takes a few puffs. The smoke shines in the moonlight like wavy, silver threads and vanishes.

'And now listen to the story of Nyar-upoko. She was one of ten girls in the same village – growing up together. She wasn't really more beautiful than her nine friends. But she was Love's child, you see. Some people are born like that – full of lovely thoughts and feelings, and they never think evil of themselves or others. It was these lovely thoughts people saw when they looked at Nyar-upoko's face, or when they felt the touch of her hand on their skin.

Well then, when they became old enough, these girls decided to visit the nearest villages to find themselves husbands.

> 'Girls don't do that these days,' says Awiti.
> 'No, they don't and they didn't when I was young either,' says Grandma. 'But they did when Nyar-upoko was alive. Customs and people change. Maybe your daughters will do it. Who knows what will happen?'

So the girls spent a whole day plaiting each other's hair. Ten different designs they plaited. Some were round like the circles in the water when you throw a stone. Some were whirls and spirals like the coiling fingers of the beanstalk. Some were stars and some were ruler lines like the lines you draw in your school books.

And when the girls had finished, I tell you, my children, their beauty brings tears to my eyes when I think of it. Even queens in paradise don't look like those ten girls did.

The next day the girls washed their bodies and oiled their skins smooth and satin black. They wrapped themselves in lengths of swirling colour which rippled and flickered over their black shoulders. Finally, the ten girls put on their bracelets, beads and bells. Some were made of warm glowing copper; others were rainbow twists of beads. People don't dress like that these days, except for the tourists, and then they only do it for the money. But these ten girls had dressed to find husbands.

And so the girls set off, a line of colours in the grass. The bells on their ankles were clinking and jingling as they walked.

And they were talking and giggling like weaver birds.

And when they reached the first village, all the young men – and many not so young ones – came like thirsty cattle to water: 'Oo!' they exclaimed. 'Ooo! Oooo!' as they gazed and gazed.

Then they remembered their manners: 'Nadi, girls. What are your names? The one at the back – let's start with her.'

Instantly, the other nine girls were jealous. The colours faded. Their faces grew dark just as the earth grows dark before a storm. And off they stalked, straight out of the village. Nyar-upoko followed. She couldn't stay all by herself in a strange village, could she?

Outside the village, deep in the bush the nine girls stopped and crowded round Nyar-upoko, dark, frowning, pouting with hate.

'You! Poko! You're causing us a lot of trouble, you and your beauty.'

'Poko, you're not a bit more beautiful than us.'

Nyar-upoko stood there, head down as they shouted at her from all sides.

'No, you're ugly.'

'You're letting us down, Poko.'

And Nyar-upoko fading, getting limper, sagging.

'We'll show you, Poko.'

Tony Fairman

Questions

1. How does the writer help you to imagine the African setting? What do you see, hear and smell as you read?
2. Who is telling this story?
3. Do you think Grandma is a real person, or is she part of a 'story within a story'? What makes you think that?
4. The writing makes it seem as if someone is talking to us, and as if it's all happening now, in front of us. How has the writer achieved this effect?
5. Why is some of the writing set out inside a box?

ANTARCTICA
TO MIND IT ...

ENVIRONMENTALISTS ARGUE THAT:

- Mining always changes an environment in a big way. In Antarctica, even small changes would destroy wildlife.

- Accidents, such as oil spills, are certain to happen.

- Like a freezer, the Antarctic weather stops waste from breaking down. Waste disturbs wildlife breeding areas.

- Antarctica should be a world park. The land, and the sea around it, should be left as a wilderness.

- Antarctica should be a place of peace. People may fight over territory if they mine it.

OR TO MINE IT?

MINING COMPANIES ARGUE THAT:

- Antarctica has a lot of oil and other minerals. People need these resources.

- Mining companies should be told to obey strict safety rules. They could prevent accidents.

- Mining companies could remove their waste.

- Mining companies could do research that would help the world.

- Countries who have an interest in Antarctica have signed a treaty. They are already working together peacefully.

WHAT DO *YOU* SAY?

MIND IT? ☐

OR

MINE IT? ☐

Questions

1. How many points of view are put forward in the leaflet?
2. Whose argument do you find most persuasive? Why?
3. What do you notice about how the arguments are laid out on the page?
4. Why do you think the author used a question rather than a statement as the title?
5. What do you think the word *mind* means in the title and in the final question? Why do you think the author chose to use this word?

UNIT 12 The Balaclava Story 1

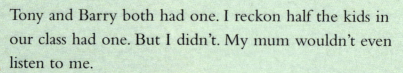

1   Tony and Barry both had one. I reckon half the kids in our class had one. But I didn't. My mum wouldn't even listen to me.

'You're not having a balaclava! What do you want a balaclava for in the middle of summer?'

I must've told her about ten times why I wanted a balaclava.

'I want one so's I can join the Balaclava Boys...'

'Go and wash your hands for tea, and don't be so
10   silly.'

She turned away from me to lay the table, so I put the curse of the middle finger on her. This was pointing both your middle fingers at somebody when they weren't looking. Tony had started it when Miss Taylor gave him a hundred lines for flicking paper pellets at Jennifer Greenwood. He had to write out a hundred times: 'I must not fire missiles because it is dangerous and liable to cause damage to someone's eye.'

Tony tried to tell Miss Taylor that he hadn't fired a
20   missile, he'd just flicked a paper pellet, but she threw a piece of chalk at him and told him to shut up.

'Don't just stand there – wash your hands.'

'Eh?'

'Don't say "eh", say "pardon".'

'What?'

'Just hurry up, and make sure the dirt comes off in the water, and not on the towel, do you hear?'

Ooh, my mum. She didn't half go on sometimes.

The boy wants a balaclava so badly that he steals one and hides it down his coat sleeve in the school cloakroom. It belongs to a boy in his class, Norbert Lightowler. By hometime, the boy is feeling terrible... and then there is a complication.

I was running home as fast as I could. I wanted to stop and take out the balaclava and chuck it away, but I didn't dare. The faster I ran, the faster my head was filled with thoughts. I could give it back to Norbert. You know, say I'd taken it by mistake. No, he'd never believe me. None of the lads would believe me. Everybody knew how much I wanted to be a Balaclava Boy. I'd have to get rid of the blooming thing as fast as I could.

My mum wasn't back from work when I got home, thank goodness, so as soon as I shut the front door, I put my hand down the sleeve of my coat for the balaclava. There was nothing there. That was funny, I was sure I'd put it down that sleeve. I tried down the other sleeve, and there was still nothing there. Maybe I'd got the wrong coat. No, it was my coat all right. Oh, blimey, I must've lost it while I was running home. I was glad in a way. I was going to have to get rid of it, now it was gone. I only hoped nobody had seen it drop out, but, oh, I was glad to be rid of it. Mind you, I was dreading going to school next morning. Norbert'd've probably have reported it by now. Well, I wasn't going to own up. I didn't mind the cane, it wasn't that, but if you owned up, you had to go up on the stage in front of the whole school. Well I was going to forget about it now and nobody would ever know that I'd pinched that blooming lousy balaclava.

I started to do my homework, but I couldn't concentrate. I kept thinking about assembly next morning. What if I went all red and everybody else noticed? They'd know I'd pinched it then. I tried to think about other things, nice things. I thought about bed. I just wanted to go to sleep. To go to bed and sleep.

Then I thought about my mum; what she'd say if she knew I'd been stealing. But I still couldn't forget about assembly next day. I went into the kitchen and peeled some potatoes for my mum. She was ever so pleased when she came in from work and said I must've known she'd brought me a present.

'Oh, thanks. What've you got me?'

She gave me a paper bag and when I opened it I couldn't believe my eyes – a blooming balaclava.

'There you are, now you won't be left out and you can stop making my life a misery.'

'Thanks, Mum.'

If only my mum knew she was making my life a misery. The balaclava she'd brought me was just like the one I'd pinched. I felt sick. I didn't want it. I couldn't wear it now. If I did, everybody would say it was Norbert Lightowler's. Even if they didn't I just couldn't wear it. I wouldn't feel it was mine. I had to get rid of it. I went outside and put it down the lavatory. I had to pull the chain three times before it went away.

This climax could have been the end of the story. Getting rid of the balaclava resolves one problem! But there is another complication, a twist to the story. Can you guess what it is?

George Layton

Questions

1. a) What is the **problem** at the beginning of the story?
   b) What is the first **conflict** in the middle?
2. Then things get even worse.
   a) There's a **complication** – what happens?
   b) Why does he put his new balaclava down the lavatory at the **climax** of the story?
3. a) Could this have been the end of the story?
   b) Would you have been satisfied if it was?
4. Can you guess how the story might end?

UNIT 13 The Balaclava Story 2

I was scared stiff when I went to school next morning. In assembly it seemed different. All the boys were looking at me. Norbert Lightowler pushed past and didn't say anything.

When prayers finished I just stood there waiting for the Headmaster to ask for the culprit to own up, but he was talking about the school fete. And then he said he had something very important to announce and I could feel myself going red. My ears were burning like anything and I was going hot and cold both at the same time.

'I'm very pleased to announce that the school football team has won the inter-league cup...'

And that was the end of assembly, except that we were told to go and play in the schoolyard until we were called in, because there was a teachers' meeting.

I went out into the yard. Everybody was happy because we were having extra playtime. I could see all the Balaclava Boys going round together. Then I saw Norbert Lightowler was one of them. I couldn't be sure it was Norbert because he had a balaclava on, so I had to go up close to him. Yes, it was Norbert. He must have bought a new balaclava that morning.

'Have you bought a new one then, Norbert?'

'Y'what?'

'You've bought a new balaclava, have you?'

'What are you talking about?'

'Your balaclava. You've got a new balaclava, haven't you?'

'No, I never lost it, at all. Some fool had shoved it down the sleeve of my raincoat.'

George Layton

> **Questions**
>
> 1. a) What is the **resolution**, or surprise ending, of the story?
>   b) Why is the ending ironic?
> 2. Why do you think the writer chose to end the story there?
> 3. We are left to imagine what the boy is feeling. Do you think he will ever own up? Why do you think that?

Jabberwocky

'Twas brillig, and the slithy toves
    Did gyre and gimble in the wabe:
All mimsy were the borogroves,
    And the mome raths outgrabe.

'Beware the Jabberwock, my son!
    The jaws that bite, the claws that catch!
Beware the Jubjub bird, and shun
    The frumious Bandersnatch!'

He took his vorpal sword in hand:
    Long time the manxome foe he sought –
So rested he by the Tumtum tree,
    And stood awhile in thought.

And, as in uffish thought he stood,
    The Jabberwock, with eyes of flame,
Came whiffling through the tulgy wood,
    And burbled as it came!

One, two! One, two! And through and through
    The vorpal blade went snicker-snack!
He left it dead, and with its head
    He went galumphing back.

'And hast thou slain the Jabberwock?
    Come to my arms, my beamish boy!
O frabjous day! Callooh! Callay!'
    He chortled in his joy.

'Twas brillig, and the slithy toves
    Did gyre and gimble in the wabe:
All mimsy were the borogroves,
    And the mome raths outgrabe.

Lewis Carroll

Questions

1. Find places in the poem where the poet describes the Jabberwocky.
2. The boy is warned about two other creatures. What are they called?
3. a) Where did the person who kills the Jabberwocky wait?
   b) What weapon did he use?
4. 'Come to my arms, my beamish boy!' What do you think 'beamish' means? How does the father feel about his son's having killed the Jabberwocky?
5. How do you know that he is pleased that the Jabberwocky is dead?

UNIT 15 — The Stove Haunting

from Chapter 1

1 'The trouble with these old houses is that they need so much doing to them,' said Daniel's mother, as she scratched at the banister with a sharp paint scraper, making curls of old paint fall to the floor. Daniel screwed up his face because the stuff she was using to remove it had such an awful smell.

'Well, why don't you just leave things as they are?' he asked, kicking at the uncarpeted stairs, so that the clunking noise echoed through the old house.

Eve Richards sighed. 'I can promise you that you wouldn't like
10 that at all, Dan! If this house had been left untouched for years it would be a mess: no bathrooms, no heating – you wouldn't enjoy that, would you?'

'But I don't enjoy this either,' Daniel said, looking around.

They had moved in just two days before. The huge furniture van had trundled all their possessions from the neat terraced house in South London – which Daniel loved – to this rambling country rectory, which he felt unsure about. He remembered that dreadful moment during Sunday lunch when his parents had looked across the table at each other in a serious and secret way. His
20 father had said, 'Dan we've something important to tell you.'

'Darling, you know Dad and I have always wanted to leave London and move to the country?' his mother said brightly.

'Well,' his father went on, almost as if they had rehearsed this speech, 'I've managed to find a partnership in a small group practice in Somerset. We went down a few weekends ago, when you were staying with Bernard. It's a smallish surgery which serves several villages, and we've found a wonderful old
30 rectory in one of the villages. It's called Winterstoke. It's really pretty, you'll like it. . .'

In Chapter 2, Daniel is alone in the kitchen...

It was nearly dark now. A great quietness seemed to have fallen on the room, and it seemed as though the house – containing his parents, all their furniture, the books in their boxes waiting to be unpacked, and the pictures not yet hung on the walls – had melted away. When Daniel looked at the stove his toes tingled and his eyes prickled, as if he were about to cry. Yet he had no idea why he should cry, or for whom...

We can't change things. He heard those words outside himself, like a whisper in the room, as gentle and resigned as the fall of leaves in autumn, drifting to the ground.

'But what can't we change?' he asked aloud. 'It can't mean the future, because we can change that all right. But the past – we can't change the past.'..

Daniel had always believed in hauntings. When he had first seen their new home he had wondered, for he borrowed collections of ghost-stories from the library and had a vivid imagination. But all the bustle and activity of moving had banished the suspicion, and the noise of hammers and drills gave no space for quiet imaginings. Now it returned. He noticed, with a feeling of sick dread and shock that he had never before experienced, that the house had grown completely silent now: no television, no singing, all had faded away as if they had never been. And now his hands were pulling open the old oven door. With an unpleasant, wheezing sound it released itself, so that Daniel could peer inside.

There was one slatted iron shelf, and the oven walls were dappled with red rust on black. He found himself tutting with disapproval, as if somehow it was his fault – as if he had failed in a duty. But what duty? He shook his head to rid himself of the awful feeling of guilt that had descended on him. Something had happened. He knew it. There was nothing he could have done, for *we can't change things*. No, we can't.

He was on his hands and knees staring into the black mouth of one of its ovens, and hearing those helpless words coming, it seemed, from inside the dark opening itself.

'Who is it?' he whispered fearfully, and waited for a reply. But there was none. Only a whirring sensation in his head and a sighing sound in his ears, as if from a sea-shell; but instead of the sense of wind and waves there was a falling, a dead drifting down of the dust of years. And Daniel Richards felt himself leaning forwards, looking into the mouth of the stove as if he could find in its filthy interior the answer to the question which troubled him.

'What could I have done?' he cried aloud, as if some long dead pain were forced from him. 'I couldn't go, I couldn't!' Then it seemed that he was falling forwards with the dust, tracing a path through the webs of countless spiders, moving away from himself into the blackness. It was the black of the old stove, which he now saw smeared on both the hands he held up in front of his face. And then he gave in at last to the smooth darkness that poured in through his eyes. . .

from Chapter 3

It seemed as though he was pulling himself upwards from a deep black hole, or from the bottom of the sea – swimming up painfully towards the light. But there was little light – only a faint glow from somewhere near him and a wonderful warmth, which made him very sleepy again. A voice was calling in his ear, a voice which was rich and warm, too.

'Come on, my lad, wake up! Come on, Dan, let's see you!'

The accent was strongly Somerset, he noticed sleepily.

'Dad?' he mumbled, not raising his head.

Then another voice spoke, a woman's voice: 'Oh, 'tis a shame,' she whispered. 'There's him an orphan lad for as long as anyone round here knows, and him still calling for his father.' He felt a gentle hand rest briefly on his forehead, then a rougher one shake him by the arm.

'Dan! Wake up, I'm telling you! If Mrs Brennan catches you asleep, you're in trouble!'

Daniel opened his eyes. A face was looming over him, peering from the shadowy room, but he could not make out the features. He was not afraid, though; the gruff voice was kind and the large man looking at him was oddly familiar, like a half-forgotten memory. He gave off a strong smell – a mixture of soil, grass and farmyard – which was not unpleasant, but powerful and timeless.

Bel Mooney

Questions

1. Where is Daniel at the beginning of the story? Where is he in Chapter 3?
2. In Chapter 2, what clues are there that something weird is going to happen?
3. *There was nothing he could have done, for we can't change things.* What do you think this means? Look at lines 41–3 to help you.

UNIT 16

Kennings Cat

Kennings Cat

Tail-flicker
Fur-licker
Tree-scratcher
Mouse-catcher
Basket-sleeper
Night-creeper
Eye-blinker
Milk-drinker
Lap-sitter
Ball-hitter
Fish-eater
Fire-heater
String-muddler
Kitten-cuddler
Angry-hisser
Wet-kisser
Wall-prowler
Moon-howler
Cream-lapper
Claw-tapper
Cat-flapper

Sandy Brownjohn

Christmas Eve

Bedtime.
Curtains drawn now, parents yawn.
Children try to still their racing
thoughts, but sleep has gone.

Judith Nicholls

A Fistful of Pacifists

A thimbleful of giants
A rugby scrum of nuns
An atom of elephants
A cuddle of guns

A rustle of rhinoceros
A barrel of bears
A swear box of politicians
A bald patch of hairs

A stumble of ballet dancers
A flutter of whales
A mouthful of silence
A whisper of gales

A pocketful of earthquakes
A conference of pears
A fistful of pacifists
A round-up of squares

David Kitchen

Questions

1. In *Kennings Cat*, which is your favourite pair of words? What do they refer to?
2. In *Christmas Eve*, which words tell us how the children are feeling?
3. a) In *A Fistful of Pacifists*, what is the effect of writing a 'stumble of ballet dancers'?
   b) Choose one line you like from this poem. Try to explain what you like about it and what sort of image it creates in your mind.

The NATIONAL WATERWAYS MUSEUM at GLOUCESTER

Welcome to the Museum

Daily

2½ Floors of Exhibition, Films, Hands on Displays, Computers, The British Waterways' National Collection. Allow at least a couple of hours to visit the displays.

Explore the Historic Boat Collection afloat on the Barge Arm and Main Dock.

Visit Llanthony Yard, Tea Room, Souvenir, Craft and Specialist Bookshop.

For details of Boat Trips telephone (01452) 318054

What's on?

During the Week

You may find Peter the Shire Horse in his stable or the Blacksmith at work in the Forge. Midweek there are often teams of volunteers carrying out the task of restoration. On many weekends there are demonstrations or exhibitions by craft workers, modellers and artists.

Phone for Info

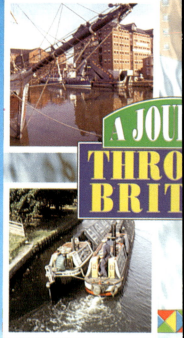

During School Holidays

Join in our special family activities. Paper Craft, Canal Art, Jigsaws, Badge Making and much more, staff to assist. With a prize quiz around the Museum.

No Extra Cost

During the Year

Major Weekend Events
Stationary Engines – Sunday, 10th May
Horses – Saturday & Sunday, 16th/17th May
Modellers – Saturday & Sunday, 26th/27th September
Pleasure Learning Courses: Canal Art, Blacksmithing, Tugs, Fender Making.

Outside Peak Periods discounted combined ticket for Museum and Queen Boadicea II.

Longer Cruises available throughout the year.

For Further information and to check availability telephone The National Waterways Museum on 01452 318054

Museum Open Daily

10 a.m. – 6 p.m. Summer   10 a.
Closed Christmas Day

Admission Tickets valid all day

Adult £4.50   Child/OAP £3.50
Family £10 (2+1), £11 (2+2),
£12 (2+3)

Party Rates on Application

Llanthony Warehouse
Gloucester

Telephone: (01452)
Fax: (01452)

Registered in England
as a Charity No. 296654

also Members of H.E.T.B.

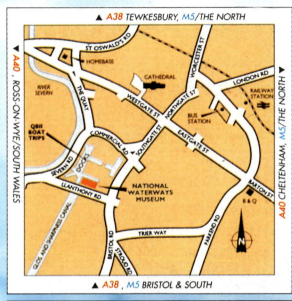

FOLLOW BROWN SIGNS   "HISTORIC DOCKS"

Questions

1. Scan the text and look at the pictures.
   a) What sorts of boats do you think you will see and find out about at the museum?
   b) What sorts of *waterways* do you think you will find out about?
2. a) Which section tells you what you can see and do every day?
   b) Scan that section. How many hours should you allow for seeing the displays?
   c) Where could you go to get a drink?
3. a) Who is sometimes there during the week?
   b) How would you find out who would be there on a particular day?
4. How much would it cost for a family of two parents and one child to visit the museum?
5. Why do you think the museum is advertised as *A Journey Through Britain*?

47

The Present Takers

Lucy's life is made a misery by Melanie and her friends. On Lucy's birthday they try to force her to share her presents...

From the PRESENT TAKERS

Melanie stepped back. 'All right, little Miss Stuckup, we'll just have to show you what happens to people who won't be friendly.'

'It shouldn't be bad this time,' Sally-Ann said like a nurse comforting a patient before an operation.

'Ready,' Melanie said.

Vicky and Sally-Ann each raised a foot above one of Lucy's.

'Stamp!' Melanie ordered.

The hovering feet pounded down on Lucy's toes, screwed this way and that, and lifted off.

Lucy cried out, and instinctively tried to bend down to grasp her feet and comfort them. But Vicky and Sally-Ann pinned her against the wall: all she could do was squirm, and shift her toes about inside her shoes, trying to wiggle the hurt out of them. Tears filled her eyes. Through them, as she bent her head to hide her face, she saw the scruffed and dented surface of her birthday shoes.

She had been wanting them for weeks. Her father had made a special trip to Gloucester to buy them for her, and this morning, longing to wear them, she could not resist the temptation. Now the pain in her toes was nothing to the distress she felt for her ruined gift. She hated Melanie for that.

As soon as she recovered her breath and could see properly again, she glared her hatred at Melanie, who laughed, as if pleased by such passionate dislike.

'Come on, Pukey,' Melanie said. 'Tell us all about your other presents.'

Lucy shook her head.

'You must have had millions,' Sally-Ann said. 'Stuck-ups like you always do.'

'Think you're something, you do', Vicky said, 'coming to school in that poncy car.'

'Other people come in their parents' cars.' She could not help herself. Why should they get away with saying such stupid things about her?

'I don't,' Vicky said, twisting Lucy's arm a turn.

'And not in showoff big ones like your dad's,' Sally-Ann said.

'He has a big car for his work. He has to carry a lot.'

'Work!' Vicky sneered. 'Call what he do *work*. Owning a shop.'

'Doesn't own it. He manages it.'

'Same difference. Up the workers.'

Aidan Chambers

From THE HOMECOMING

Hari and his sister Lila are the eldest children of an Indian family. When their mother falls ill, and their father is out of work, Hari has to go to Bombay to get a job. Lila is left to look after her two sisters, Bela and Kamal. This extract describes Hari's return home.

'Lila, Bela, Kamal!' he called.
In an instant Lila was at the door, her old purple sari gathered about her, her face peeping out, brown and curious. When she saw him, she gasped. They stared at each other. Then she ran out crying, 'Hari! Hari, I knew you would come. It's Diwali tomorrow and I knew you'd come!'

'How did you know? I didn't write.'

'Oh, I knew, I knew you would,' Lila smiled. 'And we made sweets for you, Hari – come and eat.'

Hari wanted to ask a hundred questions, all at once, about their mother, their father, Bela and Kamal, about the village and Biju's boat and everything. Instead he followed Lila into the house. Old and shabby it might be, but how shady and cool it was. He felt grateful for it, just as it was, and stood breathing in its air silently. Only the invisible pigeons could be heard, letting flow their musical notes like soft, feathered bubbles trickling through the air.

Then Lila came towards him with a brass tray on the palm of her hand. It was heaped with the sweets she had made of rice powder and cream, sugar and flour and semolina and coconut.

Hari said, 'But I must wash first: I am dusty.' He went out by the back door where the big earthenware jar stood filled with water from the well and tipping it over he washed his face and hands, sprinkling some of the cool water on his hair as well. He felt that in all the nine months that he had spent in Bombay he had not had a wash as cool and refreshing as this.

When he turned, Lila was standing in the doorway with a towel and he took it from her and wiped himself.

'How good the water feels here,' he said.

'Our well is sweet, you know, she said, smiling.

'But so sweet – I had forgotten.' He shook his head, making drops fly. 'I forgot too much Lila, where's mother?' He did not dare look at her face for fear there would be a sign on it of bad news, but Lila looked back at him steadily.

'Mother is away in hospital, in Alibagh. The de Silvas took her there in the car. I go to see her sometimes, when I have the bus fare. She is much better.'

'How – ?'

'With good food and proper medicine, I suppose. The doctor said it was anaemia which she got because of having poor food to eat.'

Hari tried hard to take that in. He knew the food they ate was inadequate, but he had not known you could fall ill because of that. Now he would have to see to it that they ate better.

'I have all sorts of plans, Lila,' he burst out. 'I'll tell you –'

'Come, eat your sweets first. We made them for Diwali, but we'll start celebrating today,' she laughed and went to get the tray with the sweets. Hari reached out for his favourite, a fried dumpling stuffed with sweet semolina and grated coconut, and bit into it greedily. It was crisp and delicate, the way Lila always made them. His mouth was still full when Bela and Kamal arrived.

They didn't know what to do next – hug each other, talk or eat sweets. They tried to do everything at once, and there was hubbub.

Anita Desai

Questions

1. Which story did you find more interesting? Is that because you like this genre? Or because it's closer to your personal experience?
2. Did you recognize the different genres?
3. What is it about the first extract that tells you what genre it belongs to?
4. Can you think of any other stories about school problems?
5. What other family problem stories do you know?

UNIT 19 Struggling to be Real

From BLACK BEAUTY

1   I cannot say how long I had slept, nor what time in the night it was, but I woke up very uncomfortable, though I hardly knew why. I got up, the air seemed all thick and choking. I heard Ginger coughing and one of the other horses moved about restlessly; it was quite dark, and I could see nothing, but the stable was very full of smoke, and I hardly knew how to breathe.

The trap door had been left open, and I thought that was the place it came through. I listened and heard a soft rushing sort of noise, and a low crackling and snapping. I did not know what it was, but there was something in the sound so strange that it made me tremble all over. The other horses were now
10   all awake; some were pulling at their halters, others were stamping.

At last I heard steps outside, and the ostler who had put up the traveller's horse burst into the stable with a lantern, and began to untie the horses, and try to lead them out; but he seemed in such a hurry, and so frightened himself that he frightened me still more. The first horse would not go with him; he tried the second and third, they too would not stir. He came to me next and tried to drag me out of the stall by force; of course that was no use. He tried us all by turns and then left the stable.

No doubt we were very foolish, but danger seemed to be all round, and there was nobody we knew to trust in, and all was strange and uncertain. The
20   fresh air that had come in through the open door made it easier to breathe, but the rushing sound overhead grew louder, and as I looked upward, through the bars of my empty rack, I saw a red light flickering on the wall. Then I heard a cry of 'Fire' outside, and the old ostler quietly and quickly came in; he got one horse out, and went to another, but the flames were playing round the trap door, and the roaring overhead was dreadful.

The next thing I heard was James's voice, quiet and cheery, as it always was.

'Come, my beauties, it is time for us to be off, so wake up and come along.' I stood nearest the door, so he came to me first, patting me as he came in.

'Come, Beauty, on with your bridle, my boy, we'll soon be out of this smother.' It was on in no time; then he took the scarf off his neck, and tied it lightly over my eyes, and patting and coaxing he led me out of the stable. Safe in the yard, he slipped the scarf off my eyes, and shouted, 'Here, somebody! take this horse while I go back for the other.'

A tall broad man stepped forward and took me, and James darted back into the stable. I set up a shrill whinny as I saw him go. Ginger told me afterwards that whinny was the best thing I could have done for her, for had she not heard me outside, she would never have had the courage to come out.

Anna Sewell

From THE HAUNTING

1   A figure was slowly forming out of the air: a child – quite a little one, only about four or five – struggling to be real. A curious pale face grew clearer against a halo of shining hair, silver gold hair that curled and crinkled, fading into the air like bright smoke. The child was smiling. It seemed to be having some difficulty in seeing Barney so that he felt that *he* might be the one who was not quite real. Well, he was used to feeling that. . . So Barney was not too surprised to see the ghost looking like a flat paper doll stuck against the air by some magician's glue. Then it became round and
10 real, looking alive, but old-fashioned and strange, in its blue velvet suit and lace collar. A soft husky voice came out of it.

'Barnaby's dead!' it said. 'Barnaby's dead! I'm going to be very lonely.'

Barney stood absolutely still, feeling more tilted and dizzy than ever. His head rang as if it were strung like a bead on the thin humming that ran, like electricity, from ear to ear.

The ghost seemed to be announcing his death by his proper christened name of Barnaby – not just telling him he was going to die, but telling him that he was actually dead already. Now it spoke again.

'Barnaby's dead!' it said in exactly the same soft husky voice. 'Barnaby's dead! I'm going to be very lonely.' It wasn't just that it said the same words that it had said earlier. Its very tone – the lifts and falls and flutterings of its voice – was exactly the same. . .

'Barnaby's dead!' it said. 'Barnaby's dead! And I'm going to be very lonely.'

Then it spun like a propeller, slowly at first then faster and faster until it was only a blur of silver-gold in the air. It spun faster still until even the colours vanished and there was nothing but a faint clear flicker. Then it stopped and the ordinary air closed over it. The humming in Barney's ears stopped, the world straightened out; time began again, the wind blew, trees moved, cars droned and tooted. Down through the air from the point where the ghost had disappeared fluttered a cloud of blue flakes. Barney caught a few of them in his hand. For a moment he held nothing but scraps of paper from a torn-up picture! He caught a glimpse of a blue velvet sleeve, a piece of lace cuff and a pink thumb and finger. Then the paper turned into quick-silver beads of colour that ran through his fingers and were lost before they fell on to the footpath.

Margaret Mahy

Questions

1. What genres do you think these two stories belong to?
2. a) What is the setting of the first extract?
   b) Whose viewpoint is the first extract told from?
   c) Can you think of other animal stories told from the animal's point of view?
3. What features or phrases in the second extract are typical of ghost stories?

UNIT 20 Cover blurbs

'Outside! What's it like?'
Masklin looked blank.
'Well,' he said. 'It's sort of big –'

To the thousands of tiny nomes who live under the floorboards of a large department store, there is no Outside. Things like Day and Night, Sun and Rain are just daft old legends.

Then a devastating piece of news shatters their existence: the Store – their whole world – is to be demolished. And it's up to Masklin, one of the last nomes to come into the Store, to mastermind an unbelievable escape plan that will take all the nomes into the dangers of the great Outside…

'Witty, funny, wise and altogether delightful'
Locus

'Certifiably funny… Truckers is a gem'
Lloyd Alexander, author of
The Black Cauldron

UK £4.99
CAN $5.99

ISBN 0-55...

Julia and Nathan don't have any friends at school; they're the outcasts of Mrs Henrey's never picked as someone's partner. So when they stumble on a stash of money in a deserted house they try to buy their popularity by flashing their new-found wealth around.

But now teachers and parents are demanding answers, threatening punishments. Backed into a corner, the children can only see one way out. They will have to run away!

'A first rate novel'
THE GUARDIAN

'The drawing together of two children has hardly been done better since *The Secret Garden*'
GROWING POINT

Winner of the Guardian Children's Fiction Award 1988

Ruth Thomas books published by Red Fox

THE CLASS THAT WENT WILD
THE NEW BOY
THE SECRET   GUILTY!   HIDEAWAY

ISBN 0-09-959660-1

UK £3.50 CAN $5.50

WINNER OF THE 1995 GUARDIAN CHILDREN'S FICTION AWARD

Greetings from the Subtle World – Twelve-year-old MapHead is a visitor from the Subtle World that exists side by side with our own. Basing himself in a tomato house, the young traveller has come to meet his mortal mother for the first time. But, for all his dazzling alien powers, can MapHead master the language of the human heart?

HIGHLY COMMENDED FOR THE CARNEGIE MEDAL AND SHORTLISTED FOR THE WH SMITH MIND BOGGLING BOOKS AWARD

"Weird, moving and funny by turns… Lesley Howarth has a touch of genius."
Chris Powling, Books for Keeps

"Offbeat and original… Strongly recommended to all who enjoy a good story." Books For Your Children

Also by Lesley Howarth
THE FLOWER KING ♦ WEATHER EYE

Cover illustration by Janet Woolley

ISBN 0-7445-3647-2

LESLEY HOWARTH

GUARDIAN Children's Fiction AWARD WINNER

£3.99 UK ONLY

'Your uncle's getting ready to walk across the Monday River,' shouted Conrad.

Jimmie Little's crazy Uncle Pete had bet that he could walk across the thin layer of ice covering the swift and merciless depths of the Monday River. It had never been done before. Uncle Pete was always doing foolish and reckless things that embarrassed Jimmie, but this time he had really gone too far…

Cover illustration by Jerry Hoare

ISBN 0-14-031329-X

(Questions)

1. What genre does each book belong to?
2. Which one attracts you most? Why? Is it because it's a popular genre?
3. What advertising devices does the blurb writer use to make you want to read the book?
4. What would you expect to see on the front covers of these books?

UNIT 21

Anne Fine

The stories in this unit are both by the same author – Anne Fine.

from
HOW TO WRITE REALLY BADLY

Chester Howard hates his new school, particularly when he has to sit next to Joe, the Bean Brain.

'Today,' I told him, 'I am getting on with my own work.'

'Just start me off first,' he pleaded.

'No.' I said. 'I have to get on myself. Once I start with you, there's never any stopping.'

So, sadly, he set off in his brutish handwriting across the page.

People who Write relly Badly

It's no good. I can't concentrate. I lay down my pen and slide the new photographs he's brought in to show me out of their envelope.

'I've said this before,' I told him. 'And I shall probably say it again. I don't understand how someone who can stuff eighteen jumbo-sized models into one tiny bedroom without breaking any of them can't copy one word without losing his place half a billion times.'

I glanced at his work again.

'Or six words in a row without falling off the edge of the paper.'

Look how he'd finished this time.

People who Write relly Badly hav

I touched his hand.

'Are these the fingers that built that three-metre Eiffel Tower out of spaghetti?'

'Macaroni.'

'Whatever.' I tapped his head. 'Is this the brain that worked out how to make his sister's Hallowe'en mask flash orange and green? Is this the same boy who stuffed all the speaker wires back in the right holes when Ben Bergonzi put his great hoof through them?'

'That's different,' he said sadly. 'I don't have to learn wires and glue and stuff.'

from GOGGLE EYES

Kitty's mum Rosalind has a new boyfriend Gerald, otherwise known as Goggle-Eyes. He is starting to act as if he were one of the family. Kitty is determined not to let him in...

'Kitty, could I come in your room for a moment?'

I kept the door as tightly closed as I could, without cutting my head off.

'What for?'

He swung the hammer, and the wrench.

'I'm searching for an airlock in the pipes. I think it's probably in there with you.'

He nodded towards my door. And since he had his shirt sleeves rolled right up, and oily stains on his fingers, I had to believe him.

'I suppose so.'

10   I pulled the door back as far as it would go.

He stood and waited.

'Well?' he repeated. 'Can you open the door?'

'I have,' I told him. 'This is as far as it opens.'

'What's wrong with it?' (Oh, you could see it in his eyes: Goody! Another little job to help me suck up to my lovely Rosalind).

'Nothing is wrong with it,' I snapped. 'It's just that there's one or two books lying behind it on the floor.'

'One or two books,' He whistled. 'You must have the whole National Scottish Collection behind there, to jam it that much.'

20   I said nothing. I think he knew perfectly well what I meant by my silence. But I did pull the door back a little, till all my English Literature books splayed on top of one another with their spines cracking.

He slotted himself in sideways, and peered through the gloom.

'Why is it so dark in here?' he asked. 'Why haven't you opened your curtains?'

I stepped back tripping on wires from my computer and my hair crimpers tangled on the floor.

'I haven't had time yet.'

'Time? It's practically evening. If you don't open them soon, it will be
30   time to close them again.'

I ignored him. He lifted a foot and slid it gingerly between my plastic bags full of spare wools and some dirty old tea cups. You could tell he was trying really hard not to tread on the clothes that I hadn't had time to hang up yet. But there was not much actual carpet showing, and he tipped a cereal bowl with his heel. Luckily Floss had drunk most of the milk, and the cornflakes had dried up.

He flung the curtains open. Light flooded the room.

There was stunned silence, then:

'Dear gods!' he whispered softly in some awe. 'Designer compost!'

He gazed about him in amazement. And it did look a bit slummy, I admit. Blackened banana skins don't look too nasty dropped in a waste paper basket, but when you see them spread on your crumpled bedclothes, coated with cat hairs, they can be a bit off-putting. And the tops were off most of the make-up and hair stuff. And the playing cards would have looked neater in a pile. And if my dresser drawers had been pushed in, none of my underwear would have been spilling on the floor.

He stopped to pick up a mug with two inches of stone cold coffee inside it, and a layer of thick green scum over the top.

'Interesting,' he said. 'Bit of a rarity, this particular mould.'

'I think you mentioned an airlock in our pipes,' I said coldly.

Notice that? Not the pipes. Our pipes. I always hoped that if I managed to make him sound enough like a trespasser in our house, he might go away. It never worked.

> **Questions**
>
> 1 | Do these extracts have anything in common that might tell you that they're written by the same person?
> 2 | In an interview about her writing, Anne Fine described her humour as 'black'. What do you think that means?
> 3 | Anne Fine writes for a wide age range. What age of reader would enjoy these extracts? Explain why.

UNIT 22 The Write Stuff

Betsy Byars

Betsy Byars talks about writing books:

1 Here's the way I personally rate the elements of a story in importance:
- Characters
- Plot
- Setting
- Good Scraps

(And most of the other things – like theme and mood – I don't think about.)

The plot of a book usually comes first. It's a seed, one idea, and
10 what I'm looking for in this idea is something with possibilities – like kids swimming at night in someone's pool, like a character lost in the woods, like kids in a foster home.

But even though the plot comes first, it is not the most important thing. The characters are the key to the story. They unlock the plot. They make it happen. So the characters, for me, are the most important element.

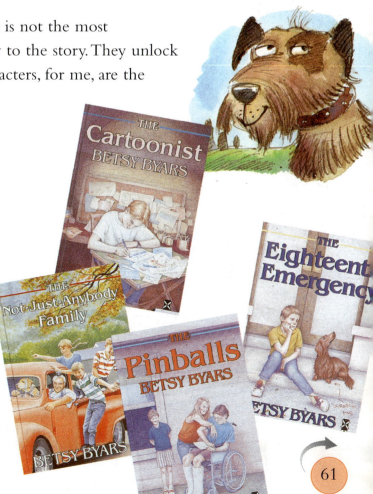

61

The setting varies in importance. Sometimes it's very important, as in *The House of Wings*, and I spend a lot of time making the setting real to the reader. At other times the setting is not important at all, and so I use a generic setting, as in *Pinballs*.

Plenty of good scraps are as important in making a book as in the making of a quilt.

I often think of my books as scrapbooks of my life, because I put in them all the neat things that I see and read and hear. I sometimes wonder what people who don't write do with all their good stuff.

Here are some of the neat things I have put in my books:

– A blacksnake on my front porch.

– A man who could smell snakes. (He said they had a musty, sweet smell like old brown bread, but Moon doesn't have any smell at all.)

– Ninety-year-old twins who were still dressing alike

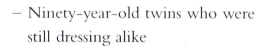

– A dog named Mud.

– A woman who made varmint stew from dead things she found on the road.

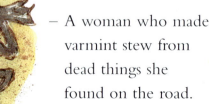

– A cat with a golden earring.

– An extra hippopotamus.

– Puce tennis shoes.

– An owl in the bathroom.

– A gift wrapped dime.

I'll pause to tell you where I got the scrap about the gift-wrapped dime.

I was six years old. We were living in the country, near the cotton mill where my father worked. It was my sister's birthday, and my mother was throwing a party for her.

Now, this was during the Depression and people were poor. When kids were invited to a party, they didn't rush downtown and buy an electronic game. They looked around the house until they spotted something that nobody wanted any more, and they wrapped it up and off the kid went to the party.

My sister got an unusual assortment of gifts that year. I, who loved unusual things, was green with envy. She got a pair of celluloid cuffs that office workers used to put on their arms to keep their blouse cuffs clean. I loved the celluloid cuffs and borrowed them at every opportunity.

There was one tiny gift wrapped in notebook paper. I must have been an unimaginative child because I kept saying, 'Open the little one! Open the little one!'

I thought it was probably a ring, but anybody who could afford to give my sister a ring could afford a piece of real wrapping paper, so what could it be?

At last she opened it. It was a dime.

And that gift-wrapped dime stayed in my mind for the rest of my life, even after I gave it to Harold V. Coleman in the gift exchange in *After the Goat Man*.

Betsy Byars

Questions

1. What does Betsy Byars suggest comes first when she is writing a book?
2. Why does she say the plot is *like a seed*?
3. What is the most important element in her stories?
4. What does she mean by *good scraps*?
5. In her memory of the gift-wrapped dime why does she say that she *must have been an unimaginative child*?

UNIT 23

From 'rash' to 'sprain'

ra-sc

rash: spots, weals or redness of the skin. Caused by allergies, e.g. dermatitis, eczema, hives; fungi, e.g. athlete's foot, ringworm; viruses, e.g. measles, rubella, chickenpox; heat, e.g. heat rash, prickly heat; or irritation, e.g. from rough, tight or soiled clothing. Often itchy.

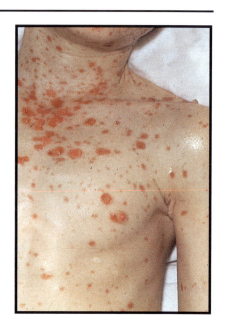

rubella: infectious disease caused by a virus. Signs are a cold, fever, sore eyes and a pink rash. Patient is infectious for five days after rash appears. It can affect unborn babies. Commonly called 'German measles'.

scab: a dried crust of blood that forms over a sore. Keeps out germs while sore heals.

scald: (see BURN)

Questions

1. What sort of information are we given in this extract?
2. How are the entries in the extract organized?
3. What do you notice about the way each entry is written and punctuated?

sc-sp

scar: mark left on the skin after a wound, sore or burn has healed. Medical name is *cicatrix*.

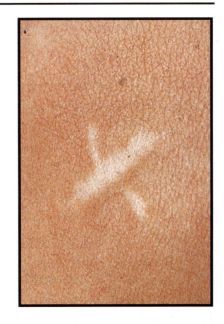

A scar from a knee operation

shivering: trembling, shaking or quivering of the body. Can be caused by cold, fear or excitement.

sneezing: sudden blast of air out of the nose and mouth at speeds up to 100 kph. A way of getting rid of anything that blocks or irritates the nose, e.g. dust, pollen.

sprain: injury to tendons around a joint. Caused by sudden stretching. Signs are pain, swelling and bruising.

---

4 | Scan the pages and find the answers to these questions as quickly as you can.
   a) How fast is a sneeze?
   b) For how long is a rubella patient infectious?

Small Dawn Song

Small Dawn Song

This is just to say Thank You

to the tick
   of the downstairs clock
      like a blind man's stick
         tap-tip on through the dark

to the lone
   silly blackbird who sang
      before dawn when no one
         should have been listening

to the wheeze
   and chink of the milk float
      like an old nightwatchman clinking keys
      and clearing his throat

Six o'clock and all's well
Six o'clock and all's well

The night's been going on
      so long
      so long

This is just to say Thank You.

Philip Gross

For Francesca

It's so early in the morning

the cobweb
stretched between the gateposts
is not yet broken

couples
stir in their beds
and sigh and smile
and the hard
words of the day
are not yet spoken

It's so early in the morning

the street lamps go out
one by one
the small stars disappear
and your life
has barely begun

It's so early in the morning

Helen Dunmore

Questions

1. What are the three things that the poet 'thanks' in the poem *Small Dawn Song*?
2. How do you think the poet feels now that it is dawn?
3. Which words tell you that the poet has been waiting for dawn?
4. a) In the last verse of the poem *For Francesca*, which words suggest how old Francesca might be?
   b) Who do you think Francesca is?
5. Which poem do you prefer and why?

UNIT 25 Evacuation

THE GOVERNMENT EVACUATION SCHEME

Why evacuate?

1   War has been declared and cities are being attacked from the air. Although the nation's defences are strong some bombers are getting through. In order to avoid panic, and for protection, plans have been made by the Government for the evacuation of school children, children under school age (if accompanied by mothers or another responsible adult) and pregnant mothers, from large towns and cities to safer areas.

What is the Scheme?

This is a voluntary scheme. Children don't have to go, but obviously they will be much safer and happier away from the
10 cities because the dangers there are greatest.
There is room in the safe areas for the children. Homes have been offered by local people and children are made welcome. Teachers and other helpers go with the children as their schooling must not be disrupted.

What happens?

Parents of school children are being told by schools of the transportation details. School children assemble at their schools and travel together with their teachers by train. Once they reach their destination they are collected by local families. Because 3 million children are being moved it is
20 not possible to let all parents know where each child is sent. Parents are notified as soon as their children are placed with a family.
Whilst the Government realises the heartbreak separation

can cause, parents can be assured that their children are well looked after, so are relieved of that worry.

Children under five

Children under school age are accompanied by their mothers or some other responsible adult. Mothers who wish to go away with such children should register with the Local Authority at once as delaying the departure could
30 put children in danger.

A number of mothers have shown reluctance in registering because they want to stay with their families. Some feel that there might not be any danger in staying in the cities. Now air attacks have started it is becoming more difficult to arrange to get away.

Don't delay – register today!

Questions

1. Who do you think the government wanted to read this leaflet?
2. The leaflet is written in a formal style rather than being chatty and informal. Why do you think this is?
3. Scan the extract to find the answers to the following questions.
   a) Why were children being evacuated?
   b) Would parents have known where their children were staying?
   c) Would evacuees have missed out on their schooling? Where does it tell you?
   d) Did all children have to be evacuated? How do you know?

UNIT 26 Wartime

Carrie and Nick are being evacuated from London. They are on their way with their school teachers to a small town in Wales. When they arrive, they are taken to the town hall.

from CARRIE'S WAR

1   They all seemed to have more luggage than when they had started. Suitcases that had once been quite light now felt as if they were weighed down with stones – and got heavier as they left the small station, and straggled down a steep, cinder path. Carrie had Nick's case as well as her own and a carrier bag with a broken string handle. She tucked it under one arm but it kept slipping backwards and her gas mask banged her knee as she walked. . .

   Nick clung to Carrie's sleeve as they went through the door into a long, dark room with pointed windows. It was crowded and noisy.

10   Someone said to Carrie, 'Would you like a cup of tea, bach? And a bit of cake, now?' She was a cheerful, plump woman with a sing-song Welsh voice. Carrie shook her head; she felt cake would choke her. 'Stand by there, then,' the woman said. 'There by the wall with the others, and someone will choose you.'

   She had already begun to feel ill with shame at the fear that no one would choose her, the way she always felt when they picked teams at school. Suppose she was left to the last! She dragged Nick into the line of waiting children and stood, eyes on the ground, hardly daring to breathe. When someone called out, 'A nice little girl for Mrs Davies,

20   now,' she felt she would suffocate. She looked up but unfocused her eyes so that passing faces blurred and swam in front of her.

   Nick's hand tightened in hers. She looked at his white face and the traces of sick round his mouth and wanted to shake him. No one would take home a boy who looked like that, so pale and delicate. They would think he was bound to get ill and be a trouble to them. She said in a low fierce voice, 'Why don't you smile and look nice,' and he blinked with surprise, looking so small and so sweet that she softened. She said, 'Oh, it's all right, I'm not cross. I won't leave you.'. .

Eventually, Carrie and Nick are chosen by Miss Evans, who takes them back to her home.

Miss Evans hurried them through into a narrow, dark hall with closed doors and a stair rising up. It was darker here than the shop and there was a strong smell of polish.

Polished linoleum, a shining glass sea, with rugs scattered like islands. Not a speck of dust anywhere. Miss Evans looked down at their feet. 'Better change into your slippers before we go up to your bedroom.'

'We haven't got any,' Carrie said. She meant to explain that there hadn't been room in their cases but before she could speak Miss Evans turned bright red and said quickly, 'Oh, I'm so sorry, how silly of me, why should you? Never mind, as long as you're careful and tread on the drugget.'

A strip of white cloth covered the middle of the stair carpet. They trod on this as they climbed; looking back from the top, Carrie saw the marks of their rubber-soled shoes and felt guilty, though it wasn't her fault. Nick whispered, 'She thinks we're poor children, too poor to have slippers,' and giggled.

Carrie supposed he was right. Nick was good at guessing what people were thinking. But she didn't feel like giggling; everywhere was so tidy and clean it made her despair. She thought she would never dare touch anything in this house in case she left marks. She wouldn't dare breathe – even her breath might be dirty!

Miss Evans was looking at Nick. 'What did you say, dear?' she asked, but didn't wait for an answer. 'Here's the bathroom,' she said – proudly, it seemed. 'Hot and cold running water, and a flush toilet. And your room, just by here.'

It was a small room with two narrow beds and a hooked rug between them. A wardrobe and a wicker chair and a large, framed notice on the wall. The black letters said,

The Eye Of The Lord Is Upon You

Miss Evans saw Carrie looking at this. She said, 'My brother is very strong Chapel. So you'll have to be especially good on Sundays. No games or books, see? Except the Bible, of course.'

The children stared at her. She smiled shyly. 'It may not be what you're used to but it's better to get things straight from the start, isn't it? Mr Evans is a good man, but strict. Manners and tidiness and keeping things clean. He says dirt and sloppy habits are an insult to the Lord. So you will be good, won't you? You look like good children.'

Nina Bawden

Questions

1. Why were children evacuated during the war?
2. What happens when the children arrive at the town hall?
3. Why does Carrie think that nobody will choose them?
4. How do you think the children's lives are going to change?

The next extract shows what life was like for some of those left behind in the city.

from FIREWEED

1   There was an air-raid going on, but we weren't taking much notice and neither was anyone else near us. They happened too often. They lasted too long. One just got tired of it, just couldn't react for every one. So there we were selling oranges. Suddenly there was a terrible racket a little way off, sirens and firebells, and a roar of flame so fierce we could hear it where we stood. The sky over St Paul's filled with billowing smoke, and then the underside of the black smoke-cloud lit up a lurid yellow. Cinders the size of saucers fell around us. And out of the doorway of the Paradise Buildings, opposite our stall, a bloke came running like a
10 maniac. He had a helmet on, and an Auxiliary Fire Service Jacket, which he was still buttoning as he ran, and he was wearing his pyjama trousers. Poor devil must have been snatching a bit of sleep. He was stout, I remember, and a large triangle of hairy belly showed through where the pyjamas tied. Panting for breath he ran off towards the fire.

'Go on Charlie!' cried a delighted crowd of onlookers.

'Had enough shut-eye?'

Cupping his hands to his mouth the barrow boy beside us bellowed after him, 'Where's your trousers?'

He disappeared into the foul-smelling wall of smoke at the far end of
20 the street. Fire-fighting must take guts at the best of times, but the fires caused by incendiary bombs were like acres of hell itself. And he was such an ordinary sort of bloke, fat and hairy, and a bit red in the face...

Jill Paton-Walsh

Questions

1 When is the story set? How do you know?
2 What are the main characters doing at the start of the story?
3 What is the dramatic event that suddenly happens?
4 What is Charlie's job? What is he running to do?

UNIT 27 Haiku Bestiary

a
Ants in straggly lines
Marching over pavement cracks,
Stop to wave at friends.

b
A tiny flitter
Through the dusk – watch the shy bat
Inhabit his world.

c
Cat – King of the Beasts.
Even a common moggy
Has the regal air.

d
A dragonfly darts
Here, there, across the wooden
Path on the marshes.

e
Eels slip from your hands
Like long, fat, black spaghetti
Down the river's plug.

f
Caught in Spring sunlight,
The finch pecks at the blossom.
No apples this year.

g
Before each foot falls
Grasshoppers fountain into
Air like lawn sprinklers.

h
A hedgehog stands up
So much further off the ground
And she outruns you.

74

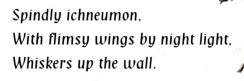

i Spindly ichneumon,
   With flimsy wings by night light,
   Whiskers up the wall.

j Two jays mob the cat.
   Their jabber clatters at each
   Scratchy ratchet screech.

k In wrapt suspension
   A kestrel ignores the cars.
   He knows about speed.

l The little black lamb
   In a field of all-white sheep
   Loves the attention.

m Under the front lawn
   A mole, with his strong shoulders,
   Makes many mountains...

Sandy Brownjohn

Questions

1. Which haiku is your favourite and why?
2. a) Look at **g**. What picture does it create in your mind?
   b) What is the effect of the word *fountain*?
   c) Select two other well-chosen words or phrases that stand out in this haiku.
3. Choose another haiku. What do you like about it. Which words make it interesting?

UNIT 28 The Bogeyman

From FUNGUS THE BOGEYMAN

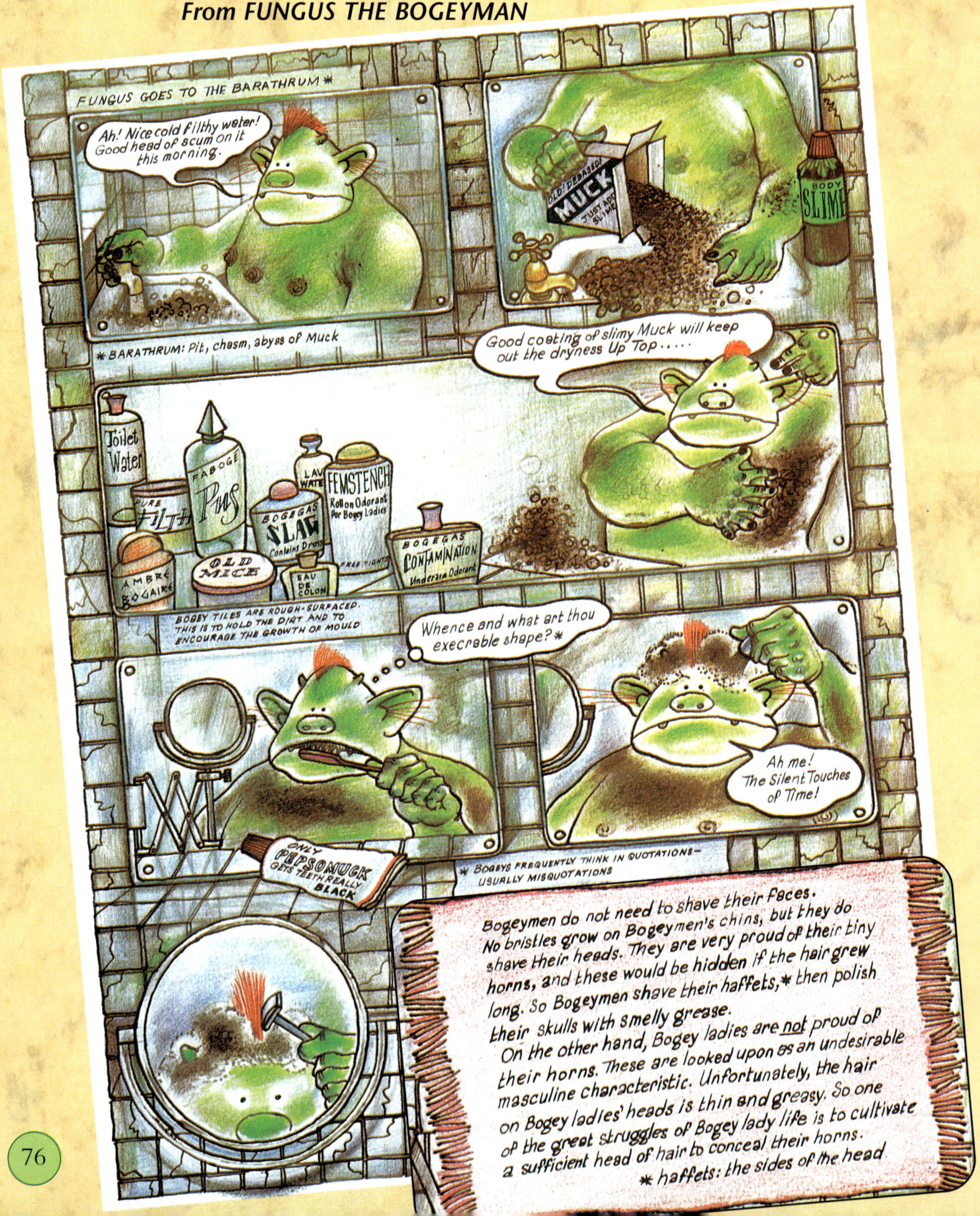

From THE MAN

When John finds a tiny man in his bedroom he thinks he must be dreaming...

But by the end of the story, John finds out that life with the man isn't much fun at all...

JOHN!
FOR HEAVEN'S SAKE!
JUST COME DOWN HERE AND LOOK
AT THIS MESS EVERYWHERE.
AND IT'S MARMALADE AGAIN!
HAVE YOU GONE MARMALADE MAD?
YOU REALLY ARE IMPOSSIBLE, JOHN!

I'm fed up!
Always getting told off because of you!
It's not fair!
<u>I</u> get all the blame.
<u>You've</u> got the perfect alibi -
no one knows you exist!
All because I did a good deed and took you in.

**You didn't take me in.
I came in.**

I let you stay, then.

**Yes, but why?
That is the question.**

I felt sorry for you, of course.
You were cold ... starving ...

You were being kind?

Er ... yes.
I suppose I was.

You'd have done the same for anyone?

Yes, I suppose so.

My size didn't come into it?

No.

You weren't attracted ... fascinated ... by my size?

Well ... not <u>just</u> that -

Suppose you'd been woken up by a naked
starving man six foot tall?
You'd have screamed, run for Mum and Dad
and called the police?

Yes.

You wouldn't have hid him and fed him?

No.

**So it was just my <u>size</u>?
Not <u>me</u>.
To you I'm small, sweet, fascinating, and lovable.**

Ha!
Lovable! You!

A toy ... a little pet ... a human hamster?
Why don't you buy a little plastic wheel
for me to run round on?

Shut up!

**That's all I am to you.
I'm not a person at all.
I'm a PET!**

ZZZZZZ...

Evening, boy.

Evening, Man.
Look ... sorry about this afternoon.

Yes, me too.
I forgive you.

What!

Yes. I do. I honestly do.
I've thought long and hard about it.
Prayed for ages.
Didn't sleep a wink in my kip.
I forgive you, my boy.

You are unbelievable.

I know.
I was amazed myself.
The power of prayer, eh?
Now, what's for tea tonight?
Any chance of a <u>fried</u> egg?

I'll go down and see.

RAYMOND BRIGGS BOTH WROTE AND ILLUSTRATED THESE STORIES

Questions

1 | What do the two extracts have in common?
2 | One review of *Fungus the Bogeyman* said: '*You need a quick eye*'. What tiny details do you notice when you look at the pictures carefully?
3 | Raymond Briggs says, *I begin with a fantasy and then play it straight. . . A tiny man appearing, a snowman coming to life. Right. Now what happens*?
What do you think he means?
4 | Some of the messages in Raymond Briggs' stories are very serious. What do you think is the message in *The Man*?

UNIT 29 This is Just to Say

Two poems by William Carlos Williams

This Is Just to Say

I have eaten
the plums
that were in
the icebox

and which
you were probably
saving
for breakfast

Forgive me
they were delicious
so sweet
and so cold

The Red Wheelbarrow

so much depends
upon

a red wheel
barrow

glazed with rain
water

beside the white
chickens.

Questions

1. If you could have written one of these poems, which would you choose?
2. In *This is Just to Say*, who do you think the poem is written by and who is it for?
3. How do you think the person receiving the poem will feel?
4. In *The Red Wheelbarrow* what do you notice about the pattern of the words?
5. Which word or phrase do you like best in *The Red Wheelbarrow*? Try to explain why.